A Fight for My Soul

A True Story of Spiritual Warfare

ADRIANNE T. BRYCE

WESTBOW
PRESS*
A DIVISION OF THOMAS NELSON
& ZONDERVAN

Scripture taken from the Holy Bible, NEW INTERNATIONAL VERSION®. Copyright © 1973, 1978, 1984 by Biblica, Inc. All rights reserved worldwide. Used by permission. NEW INTERNATIONAL VERSION® and NIV® are registered trademarks of Biblica, Inc. Use of either trademark for the offering of goods or services requires the prior written consent of Biblica US, Inc.

This book is a work of non-fiction. Unless otherwise noted, the author and the publisher make no explicit guarantees as to the accuracy of the information contained in this book and in some cases, names of people and places have been altered to protect their privacy.

WestBow Press books may be ordered through booksellers or by contacting:

WestBow Press
A Division of Thomas Nelson & Zondervan
1663 Liberty Drive
Bloomington, IN 47403
www.westbowpress.com
1 (866) 928-1240

Because of the dynamic nature of the Internet, any web addresses or links contained in this book may have changed since publication and may no longer be valid. The views expressed in this work are solely those of the author and do not necessarily reflect the views of the publisher, and the publisher hereby disclaims any responsibility for them.

Any people depicted in stock imagery provided by Thinkstock are models, and such images are being used for illustrative purposes only. Certain stock imagery © Thinkstock.

ISBN: 978-1-5127-2991-7 (sc)
ISBN: 978-1-5127-2990-0 (e)

Library of Congress Control Number: 2016901890

Print information available on the last page.

WestBow Press rev. date: 2/16/2016

Contents

Prologue

"The thief comes only to steal and kill and destroy; I have come that they may have life, and have it to the full" (John 10:10 NIV). I found this out in the autumn of 2005. This book highlights the events of my life up to and since I became a born-again Christian. I chose this title because the spiritual warfare I have experienced has been a fight for my soul. The fight might not be over, but the good news is that the Lord is winning.

Chapter 1

Childhood

I was born in 1964. I had a mom, a dad, and a brother whom I adored. We lived on a farm in Iowa. It was a beautiful two-hundred-acre piece of land. The farm had a large, white farmhouse with old wood siding and other outbuildings. When I was a little girl, the house only had plumbing in the kitchen. We had an outhouse that served its purpose well. I was in kindergarten when indoor plumbing was finally installed in the whole house.

The house was surrounded by a large yard with a tree swing in the corner. The tree that held the swing had to be at least one hundred years old. The swing was made out of a chain and a board. The cook shed stood to the east of the house and contained the wringer washer that my mom used year round until the plumbing was installed. As a little girl, it seemed like my mom was out there all the time. Now those old wringer washers are found in antique shops.

A large square of cement was in front of the kitchen door with a long, attached sidewalk that led to the edge of the yard. When I rode my bike, I could not maneuver through gravel very well, so I went up and down that sidewalk. When I wasn't riding my bike, I was in the swing or jumping rope. I loved playing outside. Out of all my outdoor activities the swing was the best. I could pump my legs and get very high in the sky. The wind flowed through my long hair. I felt as if I was flying through the air.

When I got tired, I lay in the old canvas hammock that hung from a metal frame. The days when my dad would lay in the hammock with me were some of my favorites. He told me stories, and I closed my eyes and tried to imagine the stories in my mind. Looking back, those were such fun times—ones I wished would never end.

During the summer, my dad baled hay for the upcoming winter. Haying was a family affair. My mom drove the truck back and forth to pull the hay up off the wagon and into the barn using a hayfork and pulley system. My dad set the hayfork; my brother, Dusty, who was up in the hayloft, yelled, "Trip!" when the full hayfork was at the right spot in the hayloft to stack the hay. When my dad heard my brother yell, he tripped the hayfork. Dusty then stacked the hay neatly while the truck let the hayfork go back to the outside and land on the hayrack. Dad loaded the hayfork while Dusty continued to stack the hay. My job in all of this was to yell "Okay!" when it was time for Mom to back up the truck and pull the hay into the loft. I also yelled "Whoa!" when it was time for my mom to stop the truck so the hay could be pulled into the barn. I have fond memories of those haying days. The smell of the hay still lingers in my mind along with the itch of the hay on my skin. My dad called those times, "The good old days."

Dusty and I had a secret hideout on the farm. There was a narrow space about ten feet wide between a hog house and a machine shed. Dad and Dusty made a wall out of old wood, complete with a door, between the two buildings. Our secret hideout was a quiet space where I could go and play—a place just to think. Many years later, I realized those quiet times were when I connected with God. I would get this tingling feeling to the point of having my hair stand on end. Looking back, I now realize that the Holy Spirit was working in me at a very young age.

School was a joy for me when we lived on that farm in Iowa. I was in a small class where everyone got along. I felt like I was really part of the class and enjoyed time with my friends. Even today, I think of my friend Patti. We lost touch over the years which makes me sad. As I get older, I realize how important those early friendships were in helping me become the person I am today. I remember that Patti was an honest and caring person—worthy traits in a friend.

One day when I was in fourth grade, I came home to the terrible news that we had to move. We were renting the farm that we lived on, and the landowner rented the farm out from under us to a *big* farmer in the area. Fortunately, my mom and dad had just bought a farm about an hour away.

My parents had scraped and saved over the years so we had a farm to move to. They had intended to farm both farms, however, that did not work out like intended.

When we settled at the new farm, my dad often said that we were home for good. The farm was only eighty acres and, out of those acres, fewer than sixty of them were tillable land. God's grace allowed us to farm my grandmother's farm during the seventies as well as our new farm. The combined acreage kept us going. We were happy on our homestead, and life was good.

My sister, Toni, was born in 1977, and her birth brought a change to our family dynamic. My role changed from being the youngest—active and carefree—to one of responsibility and babysitting.

My mom had a miserable pregnancy with Toni. July was very hot, and Toni was more than two weeks overdue. The delivery was difficult. Mom was in labor for hours before the doctor realized that the cord was wrapped around the baby's neck four times. We almost lost both Mom and Toni that night. God was with them and provided an experienced doctor. The doctor was able to cut the cord so the baby wasn't suffocated in the birth canal.

I was twelve years old and was headed toward junior high. Dusty had graduated from high school and was ready to go to college. The timing was such that the three of us never lived under the same roof for any extended time. Dusty and Toni did not get the opportunity to know each other the way I had with each one of them. When Toni graduated eighteen years later, Mom said she had had children in public school for more than thirty years and that she had seen many changes over those three decades.

Farm life was sustainable until 1979. My grandma passed away that summer. Grandma's property was sold and divided up. That meant the extra income from Grandma's farm would merely be a benefit of the past. Dad had one year left on the lease of grandma's farm and, by all rights, he could have farmed the land one more year. In order to keep peace in my mom's family, my dad let the lease go so the farm could be sold. Anyone who knows about farming will tell you that losing tillable acres is devastating to a farmer.

Grandma's death was a blow to everyone in the family. My family learned the hard way that some people take advantage of others during their dark days. The week that followed my grandma's death was bleak. My dad had more than thirty hogs ready to go to market. The farm payment on our farm was due, and, with Grandma's sudden death, Dad wasn't able to get the hogs to the hog-buying station. We came home from the funeral to find that the hogs had been stolen. Someone knew that we would be gone all day and took advantage of the situation. My parents could see the tire tracks of the vehicle that had hauled away our hogs. My mom and dad were just sick about it. The hogs were gone, along with the ability to make the farm payment on the new farm. I believe it was one of the few times in my life that I saw my dad cry.

Following this episode, my dad always parked machinery in front of the hog house or the barn. He figured if anyone wanted to steal something from us again, he would have to work harder for the goods. We never figured out who stole them, but, over the years, my parents have shared their suspicions.

Moving to a new home was exciting. I had many new places on the new farm to explore. Starting at a new school was not as exciting. My new school was a lot different from the school by our old farm. The new school was larger and had a greater number of classmates. The cliques were already established by the time I moved in the middle of fourth grade. I remember feeling as if I did not belong. Plus, I started struggling with acne and was treated very unkindly by my classmates. I felt hopeless much of the time.

When things started getting rough on the farm, my parents were unable to pay for medical insurance. No insurance meant zero doctor appointments unless we were dying. As I got older, the acne problem got worse. I was not able to go to a doctor until I had a job of my own and could pay the bill myself. By the time I was able to afford it, my acne was beyond help. Today I still deal with skin issues and know it stems back to those earlier years. I guess it is one of those crosses I will bear until I meet the Lord face-to-face.

Junior high was a miserable time in my life. Money was very tight on the farm, and even haircuts were a luxury. My hair always looked overgrown, and I was still battling my skin issues. Several of the kids at school liked to take advantage of my issues and use them to their advantage. Mean classmates called me names and made fun of me in front of *popular* kids so they could make themselves look better. One classmate came up with the name *Shep*, which was short for sheepdog. Every time they called me that name, I felt a stab in my heart.

These experiences caused my confidence level to sink. I felt as if that time in my life would never end. I developed feelings of hatred toward those people. This hatred is something that I am still working on with the Lord's help. I pray that I will be able to forgive them one day. Right now, my wounds are so deep I do not feel the compassion or empathy toward them that I know I should.

While my parents were struggling on the farm, I was able to find two part-time jobs. My first job was at a restaurant. I made seven dollars and twenty-nine cents a night plus tips. I started that job when I was a freshman in high school.

I was elated. I realized that I would be able to buy my own clothes. Up until that point, I had had five shirts and five pairs of pants for school. My wardrobe had been limited due to my parents' financial struggle on the farm. My limited wardrobe had also added to my unhappiness, as it led to further teasing by unkind school kids. Having an income was a big plus in my life.

I enjoyed my time at the restaurant. The owners, Robert and James, were good to me, and it meant a lot to me during those years. I didn't realize the impact the job had had on me until later in life. It was truly a job that shaped my character.

It taught me patience, responsibility, and respect. The job also helped me hone my math skills. I learned to add and subtract in my head, count change, and count change back to customers. My own children marvel at my mental math abilities. Thanks to my years at the restaurant, I am able to compute quickly and accurately.

My second job was at the mini-mart in town. I was a sophomore when I started that job. One day my friend Kaci and I had gone into the store for a Pepsi after school. There had been a help wanted sign in the window. Kaci had wanted to apply and had asked for an application. She had also encouraged me to apply. I had reluctantly asked for and had filled out an application. I had turned it back in and had been hired a week later. I was surprised that I had been hired but had come to the conclusion that the manager had hired me because I had been one of the only ones who had been nice to her daughter when they had first moved to town.

I learned that it pays to be nice to others. The Bible even says:

> Therefore, O king, be pleased to accept my advice: Renounce your sins by doing what is right, and your wickedness by being kind to the oppressed. It may be that then your prosperity will continue. (Dan. 4:27)

The job taught me time management. I decided to keep my job at the restaurant along with my job at the mini-mart.

I was also very active in high school. I was able to participate in band, speech, and cheerleading. All that activity taught me how to prioritize, plan, and organize. I look back now and realize how important both jobs were to the development of my character. I learned many skills that I have used in my adult life. Those jobs also allowed me to meet and appreciate the good people in my life. I learned to work with others and that other people have a lot of baggage in their own lives.

The money I earned from those two jobs helped me to be able to function somewhat like a normal teenager. I was able to buy clothes that helped me fit in. I was also able to buy gas for my car. That enabled me to cruise around like the rest of the teenagers. Senior pictures were also a major purchase that I could afford. If I had not worked both of those jobs, all of those luxuries would not have been available to me.

When I started college, I quit my restaurant job. Occasionally I went back to help when they were in a pinch. I kept my job at the mini-mart through college. It helped me get through a four-year program with the addition of student loans. I quit the mini-mart job after I finished college and started teaching. I really enjoyed both of my jobs. They just were not jobs that I could raise a family on. God had a bigger plan for me.

Chapter 2

Family

God truly blessed me with a family. I married a wonderful man in July of 1988. We are still growing and going strong. Joe and I have been through a lot together, just like every other married couple. I think the key to our success is that we communicate. Joe would say that the key to our success is a blessing from God.

Over the course of our marriage, we have always been attacked financially by the Enemy, as are so many other couples. When we were first married, we lived on my teacher's salary and Joe's pay as a parts and service manager at a local dealership. I had hefty student loan payments, and we both drove a distance to work, which resulted in high car expenses. Like other young couples, our budget was tight. Our first child was born nine and a half months after we were married. The pregnancy was a surprise but also truly was a blessing from the Lord. At that point, Joe knew that he had to look for a better paying job.

Joe found a job building forklifts. This job paid better but with it came numerous rounds of layoffs. Eventually the plant closed. Over one hundred people lost their jobs as a result. As time passed, Joe worked at other jobs. Those jobs came with more layoffs and unstable medical insurance coverage. During the course of one year, we had coverage with three different medical insurance companies. I wanted another child, but it was difficult when we changed insurance companies so many times.

Our son was finally born in 1993—again another blessing from the Lord. Our family was now complete. We had a healthy girl and a healthy boy. Financially we still struggled. We would be going strong and then a layoff would hit. It wasn't until 2005, when Joe worked full time with the military, that we were able to have stable finances and insurance.

In the autumn of 1999, I decided to go back to school and earn my master's degree in education. I graduated with a master of education in May 2002. Going back to graduate school meant more student loans. I had just paid off my bachelor of arts and had to start all over; however, it was worth the money. I have been able to use my master's degree in unique ways. I taught college courses at a local university and worked as an educational consultant for a global educational software company. Currently, I am an online instructor for a major university.

I have always enjoyed my second job as a college instructor. I have met amazing people through this work.

Some of these people have helped me a lot during my spiritual warfare. God has always put the right people in my path at the right time.

Our major blessing in 1989 was my daughter Miley. She was such a happy, active child. Her attitude and happiness always lit up the room no matter where she was. When Miley was about four months old, she developed a port-wine stain on her left leg. Fortunately, it was on the back on her leg and mostly on her thigh. In 1995, she started to receive laser treatments on her leg. This went on for eight years. Miley had over twenty laser treatments.

It was quite a process to have it done. We traveled to a university medical school for the treatments. Grandpa always went along to help. His humor kept Miley going, and he always had a smile on his face to make Miley smile when she woke up in pain from the procedure. When it was time to leave Grandpa made sure Miley's ice packs were cold enough and would push her in her wheelchair to the hospital entrance after she was released. I would trek across campus and bring the car closer to the entrance while Grandpa would wait with Miley. Those days were special bonding times for Miley and Grandpa. Grandpa reminisced about those trips for years. Today the port-wine stain is still there but it is very light.

Miley grew up to be a beautiful person. When I grew up, I was bullied because of my looks and weight. Miley was just the opposite. She had good looks and a slender body. As a result, many girls were jealous of her and bullied her for it. God uses these moments to teach us lessons. My daughter's experiences were a tough lesson for me. I realized that all people go through difficult times.

Miley ended up earning a bachelor of science in Nuclear Medicine Technologies. She got married in 2012 to a nice guy—the type of guy you dream of marrying your daughter. Miley has a wonderful job and enjoys life. She is a born-again Christian, and, as any Christian knows, it is a good feeling when your child is saved.

Gavin was born in 1993. He was an active child, even more than Miley ever was. Gavin was born with a heart murmur. A vein that went from his heart to his lung was too long. As he got older, Gavin grew out of the murmur.

Gavin went through a time in his life where he was always angry. He yelled at his dad and me about everything from friends to schoolwork. When Gavin started junior high, I took him to a youth group in a neighboring town. During that time, God was working in his heart. Gavin and I traveled to Minnesota before he entered ninth grade. We visited my friend Brittany, who had been helping me through a rough spiritual journey.

Gavin and I were at the Mall of America during that trip. A man came up to Gavin and asked him if he knew Jesus. Gavin told him that he did know Jesus. Later, on the way home, Gavin said that he had accepted Christ about six months earlier. Gavin had asked Jesus to be his Savior. When I heard Gavin utter those words I felt fifty pounds lighter. A weight was lifted off my shoulders. I realized that I had been praying for Gavin's salvation. I also realized that his anger issues were diminishing. I had a tingling feeling all over. What a wonderful feeling it was. I believe that tingling was the Holy Spirit working in our lives. Since that time, Gavin has developed into a young man who has his head on straight. He is a good-natured and easygoing young man. Gavin graduated with his bachelor of arts in Management Information Systems and is building a new life. It is such an exciting time in his life.

Watching my own two children become Christians has taught me how important family really is and how much I deeply love each one of them.

Chapter 3

October 5, 2005

The year began with Joe securing a full-time job in the military. There were no more layoffs. That was a huge relief; however, I was one becoming bitter and impatient with my family. I was not happy in life and took it out on my husband and kids. I would yell if things were not finished in what I thought was a reasonable amount of time. I was bitter about not having a nice house. Joe and I had been married for seventeen years, and I had the notion that we should have had a totally remodeled house or had built a new one by now. I look back on this time and realize how unrealistic that was. The combination of the earlier medical bills and layoffs would have made that impossible.

We decided to celebrate my husband's permanent, full-time job by taking the kids on a big vacation. At the time, Miley was sixteen and Gavin was twelve. When July rolled around, Joe came home and told us that one airline was offering huge discounts for military families. The discount allowed us to book a trip to Hawaii. We decided to take our vacation over Christmas break in order to have enough time off from our jobs and so the kids would not have to miss school.

Our flights were set, and we spent the next month securing hotels and planning activities. August and September came and went quickly. The kids were back at school and were as busy as ever. Miley was a high school football cheerleader, so on Friday nights, we went to the high school football games to watch her cheer. Gavin was in the seventh grade and was playing junior high football. During the week I was either driving the kids to or from practice. It seemed that if I was not chauffeuring then I was at a junior high or high school football game. Life was definitely busy.

Dana, the school librarian, and I had developed a close and strong friendship over the years because we had worked at the same school. Dana always liked to share good books that she read. When she read one that she knew I would like, she let me borrow it.

It was the very beginning of October. On a Monday, I stopped at the library after school to touch base with Dana. Dana told me about a book she had found at her town's public library. She had read the book the previous weekend. She explained to me that she would read awhile, put the book down, and then do some housework. Then Dana would read more and put the book down again. The book had had a certain draw to it. When she had put it down, she had needed to process it before she had been able to read more. Dana insisted that it was a book that I had to read, and, that when

I read it, I would be on my knees making my life right with God. The book sounded interesting to me, and I told Dana I would like to read it.

Dana let me borrow the book. The book was about hell. She had it checked out of the library so I knew that she had to have it back in a reasonable amount of time.

I was waiting by my children's school on Wednesday, October 5. Both kids had practice, so I waited patiently. I usually brought along work to do or a good book to read. That night I had the book about hell with me. I took it out and started to read it. Dana was right. It was a book that was hard to put down once you started to read it.

Later when the kids got into the car, I put the book away and drove home. I did not want the kids to get scared from the title or read it until I knew what was in the book. When we got home, Gavin immediately went outside to practice football, and Miley went up to her room to work on homework. I sat at the kitchen table and read the book. I noticed that reading the book had a physical effect on my body. My heart beat faster and louder as I read what the author described in her book. My throat was dry, and my mind was swirling with thoughts of what was written in that book.

At one point in the book, the author encouraged readers to accept Jesus. I stopped reading and went into the living room. I knelt by the couch and said a prayer to God. I told Him that I was a sinner and asked Him to forgive my sins. In my prayer, I asked Jesus to come into my heart. I felt a sense of relief after I said that prayer. Peace came over me. My heart rate was back to normal as I stood up.

The book drew me back to it. I read a little while longer. During that reading, I kept thinking that I did not have to worry about death anymore. I had made my peace with God, and my place was secure in heaven. I also thought that when people swear at others they really do not understand the full impact of what they are saying.

I read more that evening. As the book revealed more and more to me, I realized that I had to do my part to spread the news about Jesus and the consequences of not accepting the Lord. I didn't share what had happened immediately with my family, but they could tell I was happier and more at peace within my soul. I knew in my heart that I had made the right move. I prayed to accept Jesus, and I felt as if I were walking on air. I knew deep inside that everything would be alright. I finally understood that whole *lion and lamb* analogy.

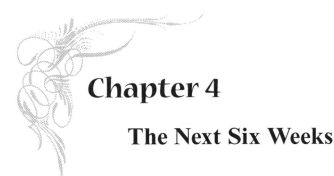

Chapter 4

The Next Six Weeks

Life was very calm the next six weeks. I was happy on the inside and it showed on the outside. I never finished the book about hell because Dana had to return it to the library. I had gotten two-thirds of the way through the book. Even though I did not finish it, I knew that others had to read it. I wanted my family and friends to accept Christ also. My naïve thinking led me to order about a dozen of the books. I knew that I was going to heaven and wanted others to go there too.

When the books arrived, I passed them out. I gave one to my parents, one to my brother, one to my sister, and several to friends. My dad read the book and understood my urgency to share the news of Christ with others. Dad believed it and knew that heaven was his destination. He was already a Christian and had a strong faith in Jesus. Dad was as excited about the book as I was. My mom didn't read the book. Since that time, she has reassured me that she is a Christian. Mom knows that she is going to heaven.

My sister, Toni, read the book and agreed with it. At some point in her life, she had had a moment where she had realized that you were either for God or against Him. Toni had decided that she was for God. Her conversion was a blessing and awesome news to hear. I felt relieved to know that Toni was saved along with my parents.

My brother, Dusty, was also handed a copy of the book. Both Dad and I encouraged him to read it. He was reluctant to read it but agreed he would.

Dusty read the book and, later when I was talking to him about it, stated that he did not believe it. That possibly could not happen; that God would send someone to hell in order for them to come back and tell others. Needless to say, my heart sank. I realized that Satan had my brother in his grip and was fighting to keep Dusty there. This proved to be true many times in the years to come—more about that later in this book.

I gave a book to my friend Hallie to read. I asked her to read it and hoped that we could talk about it after she finished it. Hallie returned the book to me a couple of weeks later and explained that she had only read a couple of pages and would not have the time to finish it. Sadly, I felt that Satan had another soul. I was in contact with Hallie for about three more years. I had it in my head that I had plenty of time in my life to bring Hallie to Jesus. My mistake was saying that thought out loud, and Satan heard it. Satan made sure that I lost communication with Hallie in 2008. Someday I hope to restore that communication and talk to Hallie about Jesus. I trust that God will give me that opportunity in my lifetime.

I also gave a copy of the book to a couple of friends of ours, Jim and Kelli. We had sons who were the same age and who had become good friends. Jim and Kelli would be at the same school events, which gave us the opportunity to get to know each other. We even went to a concert together. My husband and I considered investing in real estate with them. Jim read the book and later told me it was kind of scary. I knew that the book had affected him. He never came out and told us this, but I know it did through the comments that he made in the months to come. Jim offered to give the book back to me, but I told him to pass it on to someone else who could benefit from it. But like some of the other relationship I had, Satan made sure that one was ruined.

During that six-week time period, I began listening to Christian music. I would drive down the road, look at the passenger's seat, and envision Jesus sitting next to me while I was singing. It was such a warm and peaceful feeling that I never wanted it to end.

I also thought about my past during this time. What came to mind was all of the times that I had almost died and had realized, at the same time, I would have gone to hell because I hadn't known Jesus at the time. I thought of the times in my car where I had had those near misses (the kind that make your hair stand on end). I thought of other times that I had been very sick and wished to die. I know now that during those times my soul was in extreme danger. I just didn't realize it then.

During my six weeks of reflection, I also started to pray more. My prayers were concentrated on other people in my life and on saving their souls. My attitude of wanting everyone I knew to go to heaven was reflected in my prayers. I became more aware of the importance of praying for others, not just for saving their souls but also for meeting their needs. I finally felt that God was listening to my prayers.

Another piece that fell into place in my life was reading the Bible. I finally understood the whole *lion and the lamb* analogy and found it easier to understand God's written Word as I read it. I read and read and read. At times, I would look up and say to God that I now understood what was written. One night I came upon the verse, Luke 12:10, which says, "And everyone who speaks a word against the Son of Man will be forgiven, but anyone who blasphemes against the Holy Spirit will not be forgiven" (NIV). That was the eternal sin. I put my finger on the verse, looked up, and gasped. In my life, I had sworn a lot. I got a flutter in my chest as I tried to remember if I had ever sworn at God, Jesus, or the Holy Spirit. Anyone who swears knows that those phrases come out and you may not even know what you just said until after the fact. I kept reading and put the thought out of my head. However, Satan had seen and heard my gasp when I read that verse. Satan was about to use my own thoughts against me. I did not know what spiritual warfare was, but I was about to find out.

Chapter 5

The War Begins

Thanksgiving 2005 was the beginning of my spiritual war. That five-day weekend started on Wednesday afternoon. I came home from school and was ready for some rest. I wasn't feeling the best and skipped Wednesday evening church services. I went to bed early in hopes of sleeping off whatever I was coming down with. No such luck.

I woke up the next day, Thanksgiving Day, with a nasty sinus infection. I had a fever and was just plain miserable. We were supposed to go to my brother's house for Thanksgiving dinner. I knew I wouldn't be able to make it through the day without medicine. My head hurt so badly that I couldn't think straight. I was weak and exhausted. Joe took me to a convenient care clinic, and I was able to get the medicine I needed. We went home, and I took a nap, which did help. After my nap, Joe and I loaded up the kids and headed north to Dusty's home.

The entire time I was in the car and during the meal, I just didn't feel right. I felt on edge, and my nerves were shot.

I had no appetite, my head felt like it was going to explode, I felt dizzy when I spoke, and I just needed to rest.

We began the drive back home. I felt shaky but knew I had to do something to keep the kids entertained to help the time go by faster. My sinus pressure headache started to go away, and I could finally cope with the noise that the kids were making. The kids wanted to listen to the radio, and I eagerly agreed. We turned to a Christian radio station. The four of us sang along with all the wonderful songs. It was such a pleasant time. I was slowly regaining my strength as the medicine began kicking in.

After returning home, the kids and I looked over the ads for the big Black Friday shopping event. It was getting late, so I went upstairs and read to Gavin and tucked him into bed. Then we knelt down to say our prayers for the evening. By this time, my edginess was gone, but I was still exhausted. I started praying out loud. At that moment, I felt a surge go through my body. This surge erupted from the inside and went out. I broke out in a cold sweat and started shaking.

While I had been praying, swear words against God, Jesus, and the Holy Spirit had entered my mind. I was horrified. I thought that I had just committed the eternal sin. My heart sank, and Gavin kept asking me what was wrong. I was upset and was trying to hide my emotions from him. I told Gavin that I wasn't feeling good. I stood up, even though we hadn't even finished our prayers, and went downstairs. My body was still shaking. I was numb all over and cried and cried, half out loud and half inside my heart. I could not understand why something like that would to happen to me. I did not swear intentionally. I was getting closer to God and would not do that.

Once I got downstairs, Joe knew that something was wrong. I couldn't tell him what had happened. After all, I didn't understand it myself. Joe commented about how pale I looked and that I needed to go to bed if I wanted to go shopping the next morning. I told Joe that I had had this strange feeling come over me while I was praying with Gavin.

In my head, I thought I was going to hell. All those awful things that I had read about were going to be my eternity. My mind could not wrap itself around this thought. I wondered how God could allow this to happen to me. I felt rejected by God. How could this loving God allow me to be snatched out of his hand?

The kids and I went shopping on Saturday instead of Friday. It wasn't as crowded on Saturday, which was a welcomed relief. I still felt awful and I could not put up with the Friday crowds. The kids and I were at a shoe store. I just sat there while they looked at shoes. I was totally exhausted and kept trying to understand what had happened. Every bone in my body ached. I kept asking God in my head, "Why me?" I did not receive an answer.

I decided to look around a little bit so the kids wouldn't notice I was worried. I found a pair of snow boots that were reasonably priced. I paid for our shoes and headed home with the kids.

When we got home, we showed our purchases to Joe. He patiently sat in our living room recliner. I crawled on the couch and expressed how exhausted I was. I looked around the room and saw that the room seemed to be bright and cheery. It was the first time, in a couple of days that I actually felt safe. I wanted that moment to last forever. If only I could freeze that moment in time. I wrapped up in a blanket and fell asleep. Three hours later, I woke up but did not feel rested. I still felt weak, helpless, and desperate.

As I lay on the couch, the strange sensation came over me again. The swearing against the Trinity happened again. I felt as if I was being beaten up inside and didn't know how to stop it. This time, I felt something chipping away at my soul. I felt more exhausted and weaker.

On Sunday, I woke up exhausted. Since the initial attack, sleep had not been my friend. I had tossed and had turned all night as I had dealt with the swearing going on in my head. When I would finally fall asleep, the sleep would often be interrupted. I went to church that morning with such a heavy heart. I felt guilty about the swearing that had happened in my head. I didn't feel worthy enough to attend church. I was ashamed that the swearing had happened and was still confused about the whole situation.

I felt desperation for God. I wanted to be comforted by God and to know that I was okay with Him. The thought of going to hell when I died was haunting me, and I needed reassurance from God that heaven was still my home after this life was over. I found no relief at church. Later that day, my husband's family celebrated Thanksgiving. I did not go. I stayed in bed and tried to get some rest.

I was home alone and decided to call my sister. Toni had a degree in religion, and I hoped she could help me find some answers. I explained to Toni what had happened and asked her what she thought. Toni explained to me that I was caught up in spiritual warfare. The Devil was fighting to get my soul. Toni explained to me that there were spiritual beings who were constantly at war over the souls of humans. Upon hearing that explanation, I thought the Devil had won. I felt that I had committed the eternal sin. I was still upset, and my nerves were in overdrive.

When Joe and the kids came home from the Thanksgiving gathering, I told him what had happened and what Toni had said. I was still exhausted and felt the hopelessness. I knew in my head that hell was waiting for me and was petrified that I was going to die and end up there. My nerves would not calm down. I was jumpy and had lost my appetite. I had a difficult time eating. I was only able to eat a few bites at a time—just enough to keep me going. I had no idea how I would be able to go back to work after the Thanksgiving break.

Chapter 6

After Thanksgiving

When school resumed after break, I still felt hopeless and exhausted. I had several Christian friends and started to seek their help. The first person I went to was Natalie. Natalie used to teach third grade with me and currently taught reading. Natalie explained to me that I was in spiritual warfare and needed to ignore the Devil. That was a lot easier said than done. I was looking for answers and wondered if I was okay with the Lord. Natalie told me that a person should not give any credit to the Devil. I prayed to the Lord and asked Him, over and over, if I was okay. I asked God for signs that would tell me that I was going to heaven. My mind was consumed with that thought. I just wanted to know the answer.

Dana, my librarian friend, came into my classroom to change a light bulb. I was the only one there at the time. I told Dana that I was upset and scared, I wasn't okay with God, and that I wouldn't be going to heaven. Dana was so kind. She reminded me that God loved me and that I was okay. It was a Friday, which meant I had the whole weekend to think about my situation. I felt so helpless and hopeless.

Since Thanksgiving, I had experienced the swearing against the Trinity in my head constantly. I wasn't sleeping well and felt exhausted. The sinus infection I had been fighting was still there, and I felt downright miserable inside and out. Saturday rolled around, and I was surprised to find a bouquet of white flowers that Dana had sent me. I don't think Dana ever knew how much that meant to me. My sister had told me, a few days before, that white roses were a good sign from Saint Mother Theresa that everything would be okay. You would think that would have calmed my nerves and allowed me to relax, but it did not happen.

The swearing against the Trinity was still going on in my head. Every time the swearing went through my mind, my body would stiffen and brace for the attack. Those bodily reactions took a toll on me physically. I was exhausted and my stomach was in a constant knot that burned and burned. I still did not have an appetite and was having headaches on a daily basis. I was too upset to eat and, as a result, lost a drastic amount of weight.

I continued spending my time searching for answers. One day while I was in the workroom, my friend Tessa popped in. We began talking about how people tell each other off. I told Tessa that it bothered me when one person swore at another person. I explained to Tessa that the person who swears has no idea what he or she is really saying. I shared that hell was too horrible to even imagine, and that I wouldn't want my worst enemy to end up there. Tessa listened patiently while I explained that I had read a book about hell and how it convinced me to get down on my knees to make my life right with God. I wondered if telling Tessa was the right thing to do. At that point, she shared that she too was a Christian. What a sense of relief I had to find out that Tessa was a Christian. I knew that she understood why swearing at someone was so horrible.

Before I had told Tessa about everything that was bothering me, I had ordered more copies of the book. I was convinced that everyone had to read this book to understand how important it was to make his or her life right with God. I gave Tessa a copy of the book to read. I thought that if she read it, she would understand my situation. Tessa read the book and later shared what happened at the end of the book. I admired Tess's courage to get all the way through it.

Chapter 7

December

The spiritual warfare was ongoing. The swearing against the Trinity seemed to increase in intensity and became a permanent part of my day. This continued to take its toll on my body. I would stiffen up and become weak after an attack. I continued to feel anxious as the horrible thoughts of going to hell went through my mind. Through all of this, Natalie and Tessa remained my strong supporters. One day, I told Natalie that I wasn't sleeping well because the Devil's warfare was keeping me awake. Natalie, once again, advised me not to give the Devil too much credit. I was beginning to realize the wisdom in her statement. Natalie was right. Giving the Devil credit only increases his power and makes us his puppet in spiritual warfare. That is exactly what was happening to me.

Another day, Tessa was in the office, and I walked by her desk. Tessa said, "Ooh," as I walked by. She explained that she could feel the Holy Spirit's presence walking by alongside of me. Tessa felt that tingly feeling that she always got when the Holy Spirit was around. It was at that moment when I realized that was what the tingly feeling meant. That tingly feeling was the Holy Spirit letting me know that He was there. Reflecting on that also taught me that even as a little child God had been with me. I had felt that tingly feeling as a little kid and had never understood what it meant. That experience really opened up conversations with Tessa. Over the next few weeks, she shared many spiritual events that had happened to her over her lifetime. It was a relief to understand that others had experienced unique events in their lives as well.

During that month, I also started talking to Connie about my experience. Connie was also a Christian and had a strong relationship with God. Throughout my spiritual warfare, the Lord sent messages through Connie to me. Those messages were a real comfort to me during that time. Connie had a sincere heart, and God used her to comfort me during the spiritual warfare. I learned that God puts the people that you need in the right places at the right time.

One day right before Christmas break, our elementary school was practicing for a concert. Connie and I were in the gym leaning against the wall. I had had a rough night with the swearing going on in my head. I was exhausted and had my usual headache. I felt beaten up and was just a mess. As the kids practiced for the program, Connie and I talked about my situation. She knew that I had been struggling and kept reminding me of the positive signs that I had received—the flowers from Dana and the various messages from God. God knew I was hurting on the inside and continued to give me positive messages. Connie was truly a messenger of God. During that program's practice, Connie encouraged me to get rest before my family's trip to Hawaii. God used her to help me prepare for what was ahead. My stomach was always upset, and I now had a constant light-headed feeling. I was bone-tired and never felt good anymore. Rest was definitely what I needed.

Time was swiftly passing by. I was convinced that my life was going to end quickly and then I would go to hell because of the swearing that was happening in my head. It didn't seem fair because I had no way of stopping it. I continued to plead with God to stop the swearing. My body and mind were worn out. Every swearing session still made my body stiffen and my hair stand on end. I tried so hard to control my mind and block out the swearing. This seemed to make the swearing get louder and harsher.

Later that week, our church was practicing for our Christmas program. The program was always held a week before Christmas, and, as a result, the practice for it started in early December. I was still confused and was seeking answers about the eternal sin at that point. I was holding out hope that I still would somehow make it to heaven.

I saw the pastor at practice and asked him if I could speak with him for a minute. He reluctantly agreed. We went to his office, and I poured out my heart about everything that had happened. I told him about reading the book about hell and explained my experiences with the constant swearing that was going on in my head. I asked him if he had heard about spiritual warfare and sought his understanding of eternal sin. The pastor's jaw dropped, and he explained that many biblical scholars had studied the eternal sin but no one knew exactly what it was. I felt hopeless at that moment. If a man who followed God did not know what the eternal sin was then who did?

The pastor asked to see a copy of the book on hell. Out of that conversation, I realized that the pastor did not really care about me as a person. He was known for being an excellent preacher, but the human side to his ministry was missing. That experience left me feeling lonely inside. I had thought that if there was one person who would be able to understand, it would be the pastor. I never thought of this pastor as an approachable person after that experience and felt awkward that I had shared my experiences with him.

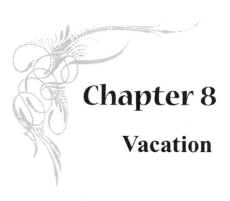

Chapter 8

Vacation

As I mentioned earlier, Joe and I had planned a surprise Christmas family vacation to Hawaii in the winter of 2005. As the time to go approached, it was harder and harder to keep the surprise from the kids. I still wasn't feeling well. I had the sinus stuff that seemed to linger on from Thanksgiving break and a deep cough that had developed at the beginning of December.

It was almost time for Christmas, and it was only a few days before we left for Hawaii. A church member had already let the surprise out of the bag in front of our kids that we were headed to Hawaii. I was the treasurer of the church and before I left I had to pay the pastor. I dropped the pastor's paycheck off at his office. I briefly spoke to him about church business. I also mentioned that I was feeling a bit better. I had actually gotten some sleep the past couple of nights, and my body had a bit more strength. The pastor didn't respond to my comments but continued talking about church business.

Once again, I felt disappointed. I was never able to connect with that pastor.

We flew out of a major airport on Christmas Eve. I was excited and exhausted all at the same time. The swearing had been very strong, which always took its toll. That, coupled with the fact that I was nervous about flying, increased my anxiety for the day ahead. I was still miserable from the sinus infection and the cough that seemed to settle deep inside my chest. Decongestants helped clear my head a bit so I could concentrate on the long flight from California to Hawaii. During that flight, I was able to reflect on my situation, read my Bible, and talk to God.

I still had a sense of desperation deep down in my soul. I wanted answers from God and didn't understand why I was not receiving them. I realized that God was allowing the swearing to happen. He was allowing the warfare to continue, and this was difficult to wrap my mind around. How could a loving God permit this to happen to me?

We landed in Honolulu at night. I looked out the window and marveled at all of the lights as the plane approached the landing strip. We left the plane, got our luggage, and rented our car. The car we ended up with was too small for four people and four suitcases. One suitcase had to go in the backseat with the kids. Boy, did they complain. We reached our hotel and found that it was not as nice as it had been pictured on the Internet. The room was small, and the beds were lumpy. By the time we arrived there, it was late. I got ready for bed and tried to fall asleep. The swearing against the Trinity started again in my head. That desperate feeling rocked and chipped away at my soul. I was up for hours trying to fall asleep. Every time I started to drift off, the swearing would jerk me awake. Somehow I had had the notion that when I was on vacation I would have a reprieve from the spiritual warfare. I thought I could hide from it and get away from the Devil. It just didn't play out that way in reality.

The next two days, we stayed at the same hotel. During the day, we explored the island. On Christmas Day, we stopped at a beach. Many tents were erected in this area, but we didn't see any people with the tents. I remember thinking that it was a neat place to camp. Later, we heard on the local radio station that the tents were where homeless people lived. All four of us were shocked to learn that this was how the homeless lived in this state. I am not sure what we were expecting. Reflecting back on the area, it made sense. There were large dumpsters and several roadside cafes nearby. The homeless were able to comb through the dumpsters for food. Seeing those homeless camps was a life changing event. I realized that God had truly blessed me with a good, solid family, a job, and, more importantly, my salvation. I later told my kids that I was happy to be part of the middle class. If I was rich, I wouldn't know God. If I was poor, I would have to steal to stay alive.

After a couple of nights in that dumpy hotel, we moved to the North Shore and to a better hotel for the next three nights. It was definitely a step up as far as hotels go. We greatly enjoyed our improved accommodations. At night, we opened the sliding glass doors to the deck and listened to the ocean. I loved the sound of the waves crashing against the shore. Part of this sound reminded me of blizzards I've heard in Iowa. There is a recognizable force in it—a force that cannot be stopped or defeated. I found that sound soothing yet terrifying. We continued to spend our days wandering around the island.

One day we went to a pineapple plantation. I enjoyed walking through the grove of trees and exploring the gardens. I was very tired that day. I had spent the night before in restless spiritual warfare. The sinus infection wasn't clearing up, and I was miserable from the constant coughing. After touring the planation, we decided to drive through the countryside to see what farming was like in the area.

We drove through the countryside and enjoyed the sites. Joe was driving and the kids were chatting in the backseat. I found myself silently asking God, "Why me?" I was upset with Him for what was happening. I wanted to know why He had chosen me to go through this spiritual battle and why I couldn't have a normal life. God plainly and loudly answered me. He told me to open my Bible. The Scripture I landed on was Ephesians 1:11–14 (NIV):

> In him we were also chosen, having been predestined according to the plan of him who works out everything in conformity with the purpose of his will, in order that we, who were

the first to hope in Christ, might be for the praise of his glory. And you also were included in Christ when you heard the word of truth, the gospel of your salvation. Having believed, you were marked in him with a seal, the promised Holy Spirit, who is a deposit guaranteeing our inheritance until the redemption of those who are God's possession—to the praise of his glory.

God led me to that verse to assure me I was okay and was sealed by the Holy Spirit. The conversation with God seemed to last a long time. I thanked God for saving my dad's life (Dad had had a serious stroke the spring before). God said, "You are welcome." I asked God if I was okay with Him. God himself told me that I was okay with Him. I knew that God understood my fear of going to hell.

I was amazingly calm during this conversation. I knew to whom I was speaking. It was as normal a conversation as you can imagine. Joe kept driving, and I was able to talk to God while I was talking to Joe. Joe had no idea what was happening in my head at this time. I asked God if my kids were going to heaven and if Joe would be there. God reassured me that they were fine too. A strong sense of relief came over me at that moment.

Joe drove to a lookout that was famous in Hawaiian history. It was the location where King Kamehameha threw people off a ledge during a battle. The place was beautiful beyond imagination. There were plants and flowers everywhere. Joe, the kids, and I were walking up to the point when I heard this horrible voice tell me to jump. I also felt a pressure against my body nudging me to jump. I realized that every time I have been near a ledge or a high point I have always heard that horrible voice and had that pressure trying to get me to jump. When I experienced it this time, I looked up to the sky and asked God to take away that pressure and the voice that told me to jump. God said, "Done." I have never had a problem with it since that time.

As I reflected on that situation, I realized that demonic forces had been trying to get me to end it all several times before this. Praise the Lord it never happened. Had the demonic forces been successful, I would have missed the opportunity to ask Jesus into my heart. My eternity would have been different.

After we left the lookout, I had a feeling of warmth come over me. I was content with life and ready to move on. I was a different person because of that experience. My nervousness seemed to disappear, and, for the first time in weeks, I felt somewhat normal. I didn't feel as if I was losing my mind. I asked God to send a message through my friend Connie to reassure me that this experience was somehow real. At this point in my conversation with God, we were walking into a restaurant for dinner. I asked God if I was going to live a long time. At that moment, the conversation ended. I did not receive an answer.

I was still sick from the sinus stuff and was feeling a sense of confusion. I thought I saw a homeless person in the restaurant and did not know what to do. We ordered our food and sat down. Exhausted and emotional from the conversation that I had had with God, I started to cry. Joe explained to the kids that I wasn't feeling well and that we were going to try to take an earlier flight home.

I tried to eat as the tears continued to stream down my face. A lady with dark hair and brown eyes seemed to appear out of nowhere. The lady leaned over and hugged me. At the same time, she said, "Everything is going to be okay. Jesus loves you." When she leaned over, a cross necklace fell off her chest and dangled in my face. After the hug, she disappeared around the corner of the restaurant. Joe and the kids just stared at me dumbfounded. Not knowing what to do, Joe told the kids to eat quickly because we were heading to the airport.

It was a while before I was able to calm down and quit crying. We left the restaurant, and I was more confused than ever. We drove to the airport to hop on an earlier flight. We were originally scheduled to leave early that evening but decided to catch an even earlier flight so I could get home and visit our doctor. I had called ahead so I knew the flights were available, and we were good to go. While we were walking into the terminal, a woman was cursing at her young child outside the door. The loud words echoed in my ears and vibrated in my heart. I was sick with the thought of what that mother had just said to her child. I had shivers running up and down my spine. It was as if the Devil had said it himself to one of God's children.

As we flew home, I was still trying to mentally process the events of the day. Due to the crowded conditions on the plane I was not able to rest and had to sit in an upright position the entire flight. My mind didn't want to slow down anyway so much had happened in such a short time.

I resumed my conversation with God. This time the voice was not as loud, but I knew it was God. He reassured me that everything was going to be okay. We arrived back at Chicago O'Hare Airport after the seven-plus-hour flight. Exhaustion had set in, and I felt numb. I was still trying to process everything that had happened, and I was still physically sick.

We had a three-hour layover and finally boarded the plane for Iowa. This flight was short in comparison, and we landed in Iowa in a little over an hour. After landing, we headed home, and I continued to have the feeling I needed to run away from something as if the Devil were on my heels.

The warfare was still constantly going on in my head. I finally realized that when I was overly tired, the attacks were more frequent and intense. I collapsed into bed when we reached home. Sleeping was impossible because I was so sick by this time. I was sure I had pneumonia. I went to the family doctor the next day. He was a Christian so I proceeded to tell him about my conversation with God. Even though he was a Christian, he was floored by what I shared. He basically laughed in my face and said that God talks to us but never in an audible voice. At that point, I realized that very few people would understand my experiences—I needed to be careful who I told about this situation.

Fortunately, I did not have pneumonia. The doctor ordered X-rays and other tests so he could determine if I had an infection—an infection that seemed to take forever to run its course. I had a virus and not an infection. I found out that it would be a while before I would feel better. Looking back, I was probably fortunate that the doctor did not order psychological testing.

Chapter 9

The New Year

January of 2006 began the way 2005 ended. Constant warfare went on in my head. The swearing against the Trinity never ended. While the body stiffening and jerking had calmed down a bit, I still felt numb when it happened. I knew that this spiritual warfare had happened before, and, if I was going to hell, it had happened before this episode occurred. The constant warfare was taxing on me both physically and mentally. All I wanted to do was sleep but had frequent insomnia.

I began sleeping on the couch to see if that would make a difference. Those nights I would be up until after midnight. I would beg God to stop the warfare and would ask Him, "Why me?" He never answered me directly, but I realized it was part of His way of cleansing my soul. At that time, I had a picture of Jesus on the wall. I would doze off and have a dream in which I was lifted higher than that picture. I argued with the dream and screamed in my head that I was not above or more important than Jesus. It was a dream, yet it wasn't a dream. It was real, yet it wasn't real. I had that dream a few more times. Once I won the argument, the dreams stopped.

Another night, I had a significant dream in which Jesus was definitely the winner. I actually fell asleep in my own bed while Joe fell asleep on the sofa. I had the bed to myself, which was good since I tossed and turned a lot. In the dream I was sleeping in my bed. I woke up and went downstairs and found Joe sleeping on the sofa. The house was full of light. There was a knock on the door, and I went to answer it. Joe was sleeping so soundly through the knocking I knew he wouldn't wake up. I opened the door and there was no one there. However, down on the steps about five feet away was a black, formless figure just standing there. The figure was not human but a black heap. The air was very still, and I yelled at it, "Who are you and what do you want?" My voice was sharp and aggressive. I yelled the same phrase several more times. The black, dead shape never answered me. I finally shut and locked the door. I turned away from whatever that black thing was. I went back to bed, leaving Joe on the sofa and all of the lights on.

Shortly after the dream I woke up. I felt an overwhelming sensation of peace come over me. I was not afraid or upset about what had happened in the dream. I looked at the other side of the bed and saw that Joe was not there. I went downstairs to find him. I found Joe sleeping on the sofa with all of the lights in the house on. What I found was parallel to the events in my dreams. This situation did not rattle me like it would have at any other time. I still had that peaceful sensation radiating through my body. I woke Joe up, and we headed to bed. Both of us fell asleep like nothing had ever happened.

I explained what had happened to my sister. She felt that the black figure was the Devil trying to get my soul. I repeated my sister's analysis to a couple at my church. The husband felt that my dream was telling me I had rejected the Devil and turned away from evil. It was a sign that I had chosen to follow God. I have treasured that explanation. It is one that I have never forgotten.

In February, the warfare continued in my mind. I became very thin due to the continued loss of appetite. People at work commented on how thin I was getting. My clothes no longer fit. It was very hard to find any clothes to wear in my closet. One day, I went shopping with my kids. I was exhausted as usual. We were at the shoe store when the attack started again. I silently cried in anguish that I couldn't even shop without being attacked. The exhaustion was increasing to a point where I could barely move. Every movement was difficult. When the warfare started in the store, I wanted to collapse and give up. I balanced my head in my hands and tried to stay focused on the shoes that my kids were trying on. Somehow time was even effected, and I was seeing everything in slow motion. Another part of these spiritual attacks was that time slowed down during the attacks. Slowed time made the torture of the attacks linger and the intensity grow stronger.

We left the shoe store and headed home. When I got home I went straight for the sofa. I fell asleep and napped for about an hour. During the warfare, I always embraced a sense of safety on the couch. Joe came over and held my hand. He seemed to understand my pain. During this time, I shared some of what was happening in my head with Joe. I tried to spare him from the daily pain that I was in. Joe seemed to sense my pain and held my hand while I cried endlessly. Emotions swept over me, and I couldn't control them. I finally stopped crying and realized that this warfare was far from over.

Connie seemed to also understand the pain I was going through. She had many connections with a strong campus ministry in the area. One Friday after school, she took me to see a pastor who was experienced in dealing with spiritual warfare. The pastor patiently listened to the story about my attack on Thanksgiving. He reassured me that I had not committed the eternal sin. He explained that people who were devil worshippers and who were against God were the ones that needed to worry. After our visit, Connie and I met other ladies who were Christians. These ladies helped me understand that God was much bigger than us and our thoughts were miniscule compared to what God's thoughts were.

I also read a book that my sister had suggested about controlling your thoughts. I tried very hard. The book did help me gain some understanding of what was going on in my head. I practiced thinking good thoughts. Sometimes it worked and sometimes it did not. Toward the end of the month, I had a night where I couldn't sleep. The attacks were so strong that night that I was at the point of vomiting. I had a migraine to accompany my misery. Through it all, God and I started to talk back and forth. I asked God when the spiritual attacks would stop. God told me that I was closer to the end than to the beginning. I mentally figured out that the warfare had started three months before. I took what God said and figured out what day in May the spiritual attacks would end. I kept that date in my mind. That date gave me hope that I could get through the attacks.

That day I talked to God helped me understand that He was on my side. God also told me that I would be okay. I asked Him if I would ever be normal again. I considered normal to be living free from attack and being able to think and concentrate on other things again. God said, "Yes." I hung onto that conversation in my heart. It was the strength I needed to get through the next three months of warfare.

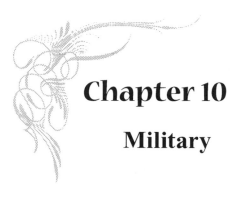

Chapter 10

Military

Joe's military career took him to many different places around the United States. In March of 2006, he had to go to Pennsylvania for an eight-week training course. Eight weeks during a time of spiritual warfare can seem like an eternity. I was fortunate that my children were still at home. Miley was a junior in high school, and Gavin was in seventh grade. The kids were a big help to me. I credit them for keeping me going. I knew that I could not give up because the kids needed me. I wanted to give up but somehow I knew that I couldn't. I carried around a sense of despair because I wanted the warfare to be over.

One day, Connie delivered a message to me from God. "Don't give up. Have patience and trust. It is part of a plan, and it will be worth it in the end." I wrote that message on a sticky note and hung it on the medicine cabinet. That message gave me a sense of purpose as to why I was going through this spiritual warfare. I knew that God's purpose was in all of this. It made me a bit calmer, which was important while Joe was away. I didn't want my kids to see the emotional wreck that I had become.

I felt a need to be with Joe at the end of March. I was able to take a couple of personal days and fly out to Pennsylvania to see him. The night before I left, I did not sleep well at all. One thing I had learned was that the Devil not only wanted my soul but also wanted to make my life on earth as miserable as possible. The swearing at the Trinity was very strong in my head the night before the flight. I finally got up at 3:00 a.m. and headed to the airport. Fortunately, my mom and dad had been able to stay with the kids so that the stress of their care had not been a concern. The one-and-a-half-hour drive to the airport gave me a chance to talk with God. Somehow God kept me alert enough to make it to the airport without an accident. It was by God's grace that I made it in one piece.

I boarded the plane with the intention of sleeping to catch up and get some much needed rest. Of course that did not happen since the passengers around me made sure that I was entertained. They were laughing and singing. By the time I landed, I was so tired that my head was numb and I had a splitting headache. I had a layover in Cleveland, and that layover seemed endless. I wanted to get moving in order to see Joe. I thought that I would never reach Harrisburg.

Harrisburg, Pennsylvania, was beautiful. The scenery in that state is so different from Iowa. I felt that I was able to hide there from the warfare. I had somehow left it behind in Iowa. I took a cab from the airport and enjoyed the ride to the hotel. When I got there, the staff told me that I had to wait two to three hours before I could check in. The hotel clerk was not very polite, but I tried not to let it get to me. I sat in the lobby and tried to make myself comfortable on the only chairs that were available. Fancy chairs are never comfortable. I was miserable and just wanted to rest. About forty-five minutes before check-in time, I noticed another guest checking in. I went up to the desk and asked why that guest was able to check in early and I wasn't. I was calm and polite to the clerk, who seemed uncomfortable with my question. I just looked at her while I waited for an answer. I realized that months before I gave my heart to the Lord, I would have ripped that clerk apart and swore at the situation. My calmness was a clue that I was truly saved. I just didn't realize it at the time.

My weekend in Pennsylvania went very fast. I enjoyed the tourist attractions and the atmosphere of the whole place. I told Joe that I could live there. I received a loud *no* in my head from God. He told me that my place was in Iowa. That loud *no* quickly diminished any thoughts of moving. I left Pennsylvania and Joe behind as I boarded a plane bound for home. My flight was pleasant, but I missed my kids after four short days. It would be a while before Joe returned home, but I somehow knew I had the strength to make it to that day in May.

Chapter 11

Jesus

April rolled around, and I still had trouble sleeping at night. Satan continued the attacks every evening, and it wore me down physically and mentally. I was exhausted. By this time, I was down about forty pounds, and my clothes just hung on me. Our school superintendent even took me aside, one day, and asked if I was going to be alright. He commented that I was withering away and that I shouldn't lose any more weight. I just smiled at him and said that I would try not to.

April 7 was my son's thirteenth birthday. Gavin was finally going to be a teenager. The night before was as miserable as usual because the attacks never ended. Joe was still in Pennsylvania, so I was the only adult at home. I was sleeping in my bed and, very early that morning, I was shoved awake.

I blurted out, "What do you want, God?" Somehow I knew it was Him. I did not receive a verbal response. Instead I saw a TV screen. On the TV screen, I saw a picture of myself sleeping in my bed and Jesus standing over me praying. Jesus was beautiful in His white robes. His hands were positioned in front of Him in prayer. His head was bowed. Jesus had long, dark hair that came down past His shoulders.

I realized that I was seeing Jesus, and my heart started to beat loud and fast. I could feel my heartbeat and my excitement build. It was Jesus, and I knew it was important that He was there to pray over me. My heart was pounding, and the echo of the pounding vibrated through my body. The image remained clear long enough for me to understand what I was viewing. At that point, the image started to dissipate around the edges. The image faded away as quickly as it had come. As the image left I could feel and hear my heartbeat slow down.

I awoke and the image was gone. I sensed that what had happened was real and that somehow I was awake the whole time. Sometimes when I sleep, the dreams are so realistic that I am not sure if I'm dreaming or not. This was one of those times. It was just like the night I had turned away from the Devil.

I felt at peace the rest of the night and slept soundly. I am glad that Jesus chose Gavin's birthday to reaffirm His presence in my life. It was what I needed at the time. I will never forget that evening. God revealed Himself through His Son in order to give me peace. After that experience, I was able to understand that the spiritual warfare would come to an end. I reflected back to that night in February when God said I was closer to the end than to the beginning of the warfare. That night in April was a pivotal point that kept me sane during the remaining time. After seeing Jesus, I longed, more than ever, for a normal life. I kept asking God if I would ever have a normal life again. He reassured me that I would.

April continued, and the attacks continued. It had been five months, and the attacks were getting old. I had the same reaction over and over. My head was always numb and anxiety formed in my mind. April turned into May, and I had a date in my mind when I believed the warfare would stop.

May 24 arrived, and it was the date that I had been longing for. I was ready for the warfare to end, and, just as God had promised, the warfare ceased. I felt release, and the attacks stopped. I was able to relax and settle into my new normal. I wanted to forget about the warfare and put it behind me.

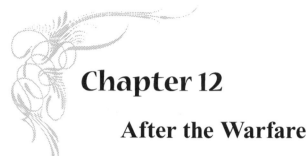

Chapter 12

After the Warfare

During the first week of June, I felt better than I had in ages. I felt love and knew it was the love of God. I was engulfed by His love. Love radiated through my body and was on my mind constantly. I felt peaceful and calm. I had no doubt that this healing love was from God. The following week, I felt friendship. Again, this friendship was nothing like I had felt before. It gave me a sense of what was true. I knew that the last six months had been preparing me for what was ahead. Through that friendship I also knew that God was by my side and would never betray me. He was my friend, and I could always count on Him no matter what was thrown my way. The memory of those feelings kept me going through the tough times that followed.

In 2008, a tornado ripped through our town. One of our rental properties was destroyed, and my husband left for Iraq five days later. Three days after Joe left, another property was heavily damaged by a five-hundred-year flood. While Joe was fighting a battle in Iraq, I was fighting a battle here at home. Fortunately, I had a very strong church family who helped me through this time. They were there for me when the time came to tear down our tornado stricken house. Those people were wonderful. Church members helped me clean up the lot, and eventually I was able to sell it while Joe was gone.

The flooded house was another story. I gutted the house and slowly rebuilt it. Many people stayed away from that situation except for my sister-in-law Jessie. She not only helped me physically but also helped me emotionally. Emotional support was crucial at that time. While she helped me tear walls apart, she also gave me the words of encouragement that I needed to keep going. Without that encouragement I would have given up. When it came time to rebuild the house, I had help from many of the volunteers that showed up from around the United States. A local pastor was coordinating the volunteer efforts. He had heard that Joe was overseas. He contacted me to see if I needed help. He sent volunteers to the flooded house. The volunteers took the building materials that I provided and put the house together for me. The tenant was able to move back into the house by Christmas of 2008. It was a wonderful feeling to have that experience behind me.

When it was all over, I realized that God had been with me the whole time. He had put the people that I needed in my path at just the right time. Without His help I would have given up. While there had been many days where I had wanted to ignore my problems I had always had an inner voice that kept me going. I realize now that God was that inner voice. He kept me going. His voice was the driving force that supported me through that tough time in my life.

Another lesson that I had learned was that the Devil will take any opportunity to destroy relationships. One day when I was on the phone with my mom, I mentioned that Dusty and I always got along.

It was now the autumn of 2010. The autumn was beautiful and my family was happy and content. My daughter got engaged on New Year's Eve. I had hoped that the joy of a wedding would bring our family even closer together. Once again I was mistaken, and the Devil used the situation to drive us further apart.

Spring arrived, and the wedding plans began. Miley and her future husband chose the date in May of 2012. That date was also the date of her future husband's birthday. What a wonderful wedding gift for him. As preparation began, we knew it would be wise to book the reception hall. We had a guest list of over 450 people, and that would require a huge place even if only two-thirds of the guest attended. We reserved a reception hall along with other amenities for the big day.

My brother's family was not happy with the date that my daughter chose. I will not go into detail about how she was treated for not moving her wedding date. All I can say is that anyone who has ever planned a wedding understands how tight the schedules of these events are in relation to all of the vendors aligning at the same time. My daughter was bullied and called every name under the sun. My sister got involved, and the family divided—another ploy of the Devil.

I harbored a lot of anger and hatred toward my siblings after the events that took place at my daughter's wedding. It was a conflict I will never fully understand. As time went on, both of my siblings demanded an apology from my daughter and even my son, who was dragged into the mess. I am still confused with that one since Gavin was not involved in the process of making wedding plans. As years went by, I saw both of my parents decline in health as well as grieve over the situation between my siblings and myself. The Devil was attacking our family.

Chapter 13

Dad

Dad was diagnosed with cancer in the summer of 2013—B-cell Lymphoma to be exact. It was interwoven through Dad's intestinal area and choked off some of his organs. I was with Mom and Dad on the terrible day they received the news. Cancer is the last word that you want to hear. Dad was so good-natured, he tried to make a joke out of the tense situation. He said, "You mean I might not make it to one hundred?" Dad's joke helped me hold back the tears. When they left, I called my brother at his office and broke the news to him. He took it well and cleared his calendar to come down and meet with the specialist. My sister took the news okay and also agreed to go to the specialist with Mom, Dad, Dusty, and me.

The following day we met with the specialist. We saw a video of Dad's ultrasound and were shocked by the size of his tumor. We were told that the tumor was in stage II and was rapidly growing. A biopsy was scheduled to determine if the tumor was cancerous. The surgeon did not get enough tissue the first time, and the biopsy had to be repeated. The second biopsy concluded that the tumor was B-cell Lymphoma. We were devastated and prayed for a good ending. During the initial shock and diagnosis, my siblings and I seemed to get along. We talked a little and appeared to have a united front when we were with Mom and Dad during this time of crisis. My sister suggested that maybe we could all get back together and get along. I told my sister that we would see. I reminded her how my children were treated horribly and called every name under the sun. I also expressed my thoughts on how my siblings had tried to ruin my daughter's wedding. My sister quickly changed the subject.

Dad started chemotherapy treatments to shrink the tumor. We were told that the tumor was shrinking nicely, and, after ten treatments, the tumor should be gone. Radiation would follow, and that would be the end of the cancer. All of us were relieved to hear that Dad would be okay. With this relief came the same old behaviors from my siblings, and they again refused to talk to me. In November of 2013, my husband left for a tour of duty in Kosovo. He was gone for nearly a year. During that time my dad's tumor shrank. Dad actually had had over twenty chemotherapy treatments and had become very thin. Through it all, his mind had seemed sharp and he had always been good-natured. Dad cracked his jokes, and we dreamed about what dad would do when he was over this cancer business. There was fishing, playing bingo, going to garage sales—so many dreams and so little time.

The summer of 2014 came and went. Dad's stomach slowly started growing bigger again. All of us thought that he was just regaining his lost weight and life was getting back to normal.

Joe came home in October. He helped my parents straighten up and fix a few things at their house. Joe drove them to their appointments and spent time visiting them.

November came, and, once again, my mother grieved over not having everyone together. If my siblings had known that Thanksgiving would be Dad's last, I wonder if they would have come together one last time to give my parents peace. The weekend after Thanksgiving, Dad got really sick. He couldn't urinate and had severe stomach pain. Joe and I took Dad to the emergency room at a local hospital, and the medical personnel were very cordial to Dad. The doctor, who was on call, stated that Dad had diverticulitis, and his colon was inflamed. The hospital sent Dad home with medication to help with the inflammation and told him to follow up with his oncologist.

Dad never made it to his oncologist. Ten days later, he lay down for a nap. An hour later, he was unable to get out of bed. Mom called the ambulance, and they quickly took him back to the same hospital he had been at in November. After the ambulance left the farm with Dad, Mom called the three of us siblings. I rushed home from school, picked up Mom, and headed to the hospital.

This time we had a doctor who was honest with us. The doctor did a CT scan and delivered the news that Dad had anywhere from weeks to a couple of months to live. The cancerous tumor was huge—so huge it had eaten through the wall of his stomach. That is what had been causing all of Dad's stomach pain two weeks earlier.

On hearing this news, my sister and her husband as well as my brother came and joined us. All three of us were shocked by the news. My dad just looked at the three of us and said, "Good, I'm glad that all four of you are here." My sister and I talked later about Dad's statement. Mom had had a miscarriage about forty years earlier, between the time I was born and the time my sister was born. Toni and I felt that Dad had seen this sibling, and that is where he came up with the number four.

The doctor informed us that the hospital did not have the equipment to do anything for Dad. Dad was told that the hospital could contact the university medical school to see if they could accept his case. He told us that medical school might be able to patch the stomach and make Dad more comfortable. Dad and Mom discussed the possibility and together determined that was what they wanted to do. Perhaps it would give Dad more time. The university medical school accepted his case. While we waited for the ambulance service to arrive and transfer him, Dad talked about many things. He told us where everything was in case we needed to start or move his machinery. He told Joe where the key to the '54 International truck was and how to get it started. Dad also told me that he loved the orange color of the shirt that I was wearing. Dad said it was his favorite color—something

I never knew before. Dad also told my siblings that we needed to get along and that they needed to treat me better. My brother tried to brush it off. I could tell that he was embarrassed by Dad talking to him about this subject.

An ambulance service showed up to transfer Dad. I told him that I would go home, pack a bag, and meet them at the hospital. I went home to pack. Miley lived close to the hospital, so I gave her a call as I left to tell her that I was on my way and that I would need to stay with her for a few days. Once I was on the road, I also gave Toni a call. I told her that I forgave her and that the way they had treated Miley had hurt me. Toni said that she wished that she would have attended Miley's wedding and not listened to our brother. Through this conversation, Toni told me that she forgave me too. We never discussed the reasons why I needed to be forgiven, but, considering the circumstances, I accepted it.

I picked up Miley, and we headed to the hospital. Upon arriving at the emergency room, we met the doctor in Dad's room. She explained to us that Dad had a hole in his stomach from the cancer. They were prepared to go in and repair the hole to give him comfort and perhaps lengthen his life. The doctor also explained that there was a good chance that Dad wouldn't make it through the surgery. Dad could have a heart attack or stroke during surgery and die on the table. I asked Dad if he really wanted to do this. Dad said, "Adrianne, I can't live like this anymore. If I don't make it through, you will see me in heaven someday." As I cried, Miley bent down and kissed her grandpa on the cheek.

I called Toni and explained how Dad could have a heart attack or a stroke during the surgery and not make it through. Toni and her boys said goodbye to Dad on the phone. Dad told Toni's boys to be good and to study hard in school. After Toni hung up, I called Dusty and explained again what the doctor had said. I held the phone to Dad's ear, and he told Dusty goodbye. Dad told Dusty how Mom was the prettiest girl he had ever seen. When he had seen Mom, Dad had known she was the one. I had never heard Dad talk about Mom in this way before. My tears started to flow again as I bit my lip. I realized, at that moment, how much my dad loved my mom. I don't know if Mom had ever fully understood how much Dad had truly loved her. I don't know if my siblings and I had even had a clue how much Dad really loved Mom.

Miley and I said goodbye to Dad one last time. I told him I loved him, and I felt my heart break. Somehow this couldn't be happening. The dad that always loved me and protected me was dying.

The nurses quickly took Dad into surgery. Miley and I found our way to the ICU waiting area. We put our stuff in a locker and found a place to rest while we waited for the news. Miley and I waited over four hours for the surgery to be finished.

Finally, the surgeon came in to talk to us, and we were relieved to learn Dad had survived the surgery. The surgeon explained that when she had opened Dad up, the large tumor had lain right in front of her. It had been large and had been wrapped around major blood vessels. The surgeon further explained that she had wanted to remove it but hadn't been able to because Dad would have died instantly when the blood vessels were cut. I asked how long Dad had left. The surgeon said he had days or maybe a week, due to the fact that the large intestine was already dead and many other organs showed signs of shutting down.

The surgeon had removed eleven hundred ccs of backed up food and stool from his stomach. The hole in his stomach was patched with a piece of fat from Dad's body. The surgeon did not know how long the patch would last. The stool in his stomach had caused the severe pain that Dad had experienced.

Miley and I went to Dad's bedside in the ICU while the surgeon called Mom to explain what had happened during the surgery. Dad was hooked up to many tubes and monitors. I held Dad's hand and told him, over and over, that I was there and that I loved him. Miley and I sat by his side for a couple of hours and then went back to the waiting area to try and get some sleep.

Morning arrived, and we went back to Dad's room in the ICU area. Joe, Dusty, and Toni arrived. Dad was on a ventilator and couldn't talk. Throughout the day we took turns holding his hand and talking to him. Dad would smile as we told him jokes and reminisced about the past. He would try to talk but the tube was in the way.

The ICU doctor came in and talked about removing the ventilation tube. By that time, Mom had arrived and was now involved in the decision-making. It was decided that Dad's tube would be removed at 5:00 p.m. When that was decided, I phoned Gavin and asked him to come to the hospital. Toni's husband and Dusty's wife brought their kids in to say goodbye to their grandpa. Many, many tears were shed. The doctor felt that Dad would not live after the ventilator was removed. Dad only had a few days to live at most. We decided as a family to remove the ventilator. Dad had suffered a lot and we did not want Dad to suffer any more than he already had.

The doctor arrived shortly after 6:00 p.m. and Dad's ventilator tube was removed. At first Dad's breathing was shallow and sporadic. A couple of times we thought his breathing had stopped. After about an hour and a half, Dad's breathing became stronger. Dad was on a lot of pain medication and drifted in and out of sleep. While he was sleeping, the rest of us tried to nap. When Dad was awake, we continued to hold his hand. Dad could talk at this time. His voice was rough but audible. Again he told the three of us to get along with each other. Each of us promised Dad that we would get along.

Miley went home that evening so she could work on Friday. Gavin and his girlfriend hung around until we left the room. Joe and I stayed in the visitor's lounge so we could be close by in case we were needed in the night. It was another night when we got very little sleep.

Friday arrived and so did another day of sitting at Dad's side. Dad could talk a little better than the night before. He talked about many things in the past and Mom. He was very worried about Mom, and all three of us reassured Dad that

Mom was okay and that we would take care of her. Dad smiled a lot that day even as he got weaker and weaker. I told him that I was sorry I had gotten mad at him months earlier. Dad reassured me that all was forgiven. That forgiveness was like a weight being lifted off my shoulders. I felt better as the tears fell. I cried and cried. Dad just squeezed my hand and smiled. Forgiveness is an uplifting experience.

The doctor came into the room and reviewed Dad's progress. The doctor suggested that Dad be moved to a nursing facility, perhaps near the hospital, for the remainder of his time. We stated that we wanted a facility closer to home. We were told that a social worker would be in to see us right after dinner at 1:00 p.m. It was after 4:00 p.m. before the social worker arrived to make arrangements for Dad to move to a local care center. By then, it was too late in the day to transfer Dad. So Dad was transferred the next day, late on Saturday afternoon, by an ambulance service.

I rode in the back of the ambulance with Dad. The two-hour trip was painful and long. Dad drifted in and out of sleep. When he was awake, he would beg me to take him home. I heard him constantly say, "Take me home, Adrianne." Every time he said it I felt a stab in my chest and cried inside. I told Dad that we were headed to a place where he could rest. Dad knew he was dying and wanted to go home to the farm. I felt like I was letting Dad down.

We finally arrived at the care facility. Dad got settled, and I went home to sleep for a few hours. I got up and went back to the care center at about 2:00 a.m. Miley was with me this time, and I found her company so comforting. I was thankful that Miley was able to take time off to stay with the family until the end.

Toni had stayed with Dad until 2:00 a.m. Before I got there in the night, Dad had asked Toni if he was dying. Toni had told him that he was. Dad had asked her why he was dying, and Toni had told him it was because of the cancer. Dad had told her that he thought it was getting better. Toni had told him that the doctors had lied and he was dying. Dad had been shocked and stated that the doctor had told him he was getting better.

The next two days were a blur. The family was in and out of the care center, and many friends were able to stop by and support my siblings and me. Our current pastor came and prayed with our family. The hospice pastor also came and prayed with our family. Having God in my life during this time truly kept me from breaking down. Afterward, I thought about how comforting and peaceful the words of the pastors and friends were in the face of death.

As the day progressed, Dad got weaker and weaker. The pain medications kept him calm. When he drifted off to sleep, it seemed to be for longer periods of time. When dad was awake, his speech was difficult to understand. He begged for water, and we spent a lot of time putting wet sponges in his mouth to give him relief. Dad's eyes had a blank glaze to them. When we talked, Dad tried to cock his head in the direction of our voices. Sunday night brought Christmas carolers from our church. They sang comforting Christmas carols, and dad just smiled through it all.

Monday arrived, and Dad was very weak. He didn't try to speak very much, and, when he did, it was difficult to understand. We stayed by his bedside most of the day. Each of us took turns holding his hand. My dad had such big hands that I took pictures of his hand next to mine. I called Dad's cousin that lived nearby, and he stopped for a visit. Dad's cousin talked to him, and we thought that Dad wasn't very responsive at this point; however, when his cousin got up to leave, Dad said in an audible voice, "Sorry I didn't make it out to your place last summer." The cousin said that was okay. Somehow I think we knew that would be the last time those two would ever speak to each other.

Later that evening, Miley left with Joe to go home and sleep. When Miley got up, she went over and kissed Grandpa good-bye. As Miley was walking out the door, Dad said very clearly, "Love you Babe." Dad had always called Miley, "Babe." That was their special nickname. Miley left in tears, and Joe silently drove her home.

It was getting late. Mom, Dusty, Toni, and I decided to stay in the room with Dad. We joked around until we finally fell asleep. It was the first time in decades that the five of us slept under the same roof. It was also the last. We woke up at around 6:30 a.m. Dusty went to a local convenience store for breakfast items. He returned, and we noted how shallow Dad's breathing had become. The mottling had started down by Dad's ankles. It was slowly moving up his legs. Dad was unresponsive. We just kept talking to him and holding his hand.

The hospice musician, Renae, arrived a little before 8:00 a.m. Renae explained that she meant to stop by the day before but had not made it due to scheduling conflicts. We told her that was okay and that Dad would still love her music. She sang some of Dad's favorite Johnny Cash songs along with the gospel hymns, "I'll Fly Away" and "The Old Rugged Cross." Renae's voice was that of an angel. Her voice was unlike anything I had ever heard before. Everyone in the family commented on how lovely Renae's voice was.

Renae finished with the song "May the Good Lord Bless and Keep You." Dad took his last breath as she finished the song. We realized that Dad was dying at that moment. We all gathered around and held onto Dad. Renae sang Dad into heaven. He died at 8:12 a.m. on December 16, 2014.

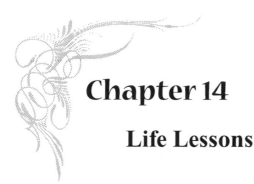

Chapter 14

Life Lessons

I believe that God put me through the spiritual warfare I experienced to teach me important life lessons. Without these lessons I would not have been saved. I have spent many nights thanking God in my prayers for choosing me to be saved. I know my place in heaven is secure. I know I will see my dad again and all my loved ones who are Christians.

I also believe that it is never too late to secure your place in heaven. You need to sincerely admit you are a sinner, confess your sins, and ask Jesus to come into your heart. It takes less than a minute. That minute is the best investment of time you will ever make.

During my time of spiritual warfare I learned many lessons to help me in my walk as a Christian. Below I have listed the top ten lessons I learned from that time.

1. "The thief comes only to steal and kill and destroy; I have come that they may have life, and have it to the full" (John 10:10 NIV). **The Devil is the thief.**

2. "In him we were also chosen, having been predestined according to the plan of him who works out everything in conformity with the purpose of his will, in order that we, who were the first to hope in Christ, might be for the praise of his glory. And you also were included in Christ when you heard the word of truth, the gospel of your salvation. Having believed, you were marked in him with a seal, the promised Holy Spirit, who is a deposit guaranteeing our inheritance until the redemption of those who are God's possession—to the praise of his glory" (Eph. 1:11–14 NIV). **Once you are sealed, the Devil cannot take you from the Lord.**

3. And so we know and rely on the love God has for us. God is love. Whoever lives in love lives in God, and God in him" (1 John 4:16 NIV). **God is love.**

4. "My son, do not despise the Lord's discipline and do not resent his rebuke, because the Lord disciplines those he loves, as a father the son he delights in" (Prov. 3:11–12 NIV). **God puts you through tough lessons because he loves you.**

5. "Be strong and courageous. Do not be afraid or terrified because of them, for the Lord your God goes with you; he will never leave you nor forsake you" (Deut. 31:6 NIV). **God is always by your side.**

6. "When Jesus saw her weeping, and the Jews who had come along with her also weeping, he was deeply moved in spirit and troubled" (John 11:33 NIV).

"Jesus wept" (John 11:35 NIV). **God understands how you feel.**

7. "May your unfailing love come to me, O LORD, your salvation according to your promise" (Ps. 119:41 NIV). **God keeps his promises and is your friend.**

8. "He is good; his love endures forever." (2 Chron. 7:3 NIV). **You can trust God.**

9. **"Adrianne, don't give up. Be patient and trust. It is part of a plan. It will be worth it in the end,"** God.

10. **"Never lose your faith, Adrianne,"** Dad.

Printed in the United States
By Bookmasters